Dear girl,

As the authors, we are very excited that you became the happy owner of this secret sketchbook designed just for girls.
Our goal is to provide you the maximum dose of great fun, inspiration and support you to develop your creativity.
We want to see you as a great little artist, therefore we contained in your drawing pad a lot of small sketches to help you to get an idea or just give you the opportunity to spend a nice time with colouring all of them. :)
Everyone knows how cool feeling is having something private, just an item belonging only to us. Therefore, we trust you already feel even more appreciated and exceptional with your own secret drawing pad only for girls.
Also, we hope that our product will accompany you at the way to become a great artist in the future.
Even if you just learn to draw and not all you are doing well, please remember that drawing is above all one of the best ways to spend your free time while having great fun.
So enjoy your new sketchbook, let it bring you as much joy as possible and help you to fulfil your passion.

Thank you for joining the group of our sketchbooks users.
We wholeheartedly wish you a lot of fun of drawing and creating many wonderful works of art. :)

Kind regards,
Youngstar Art Supplies
- Publishing Team -

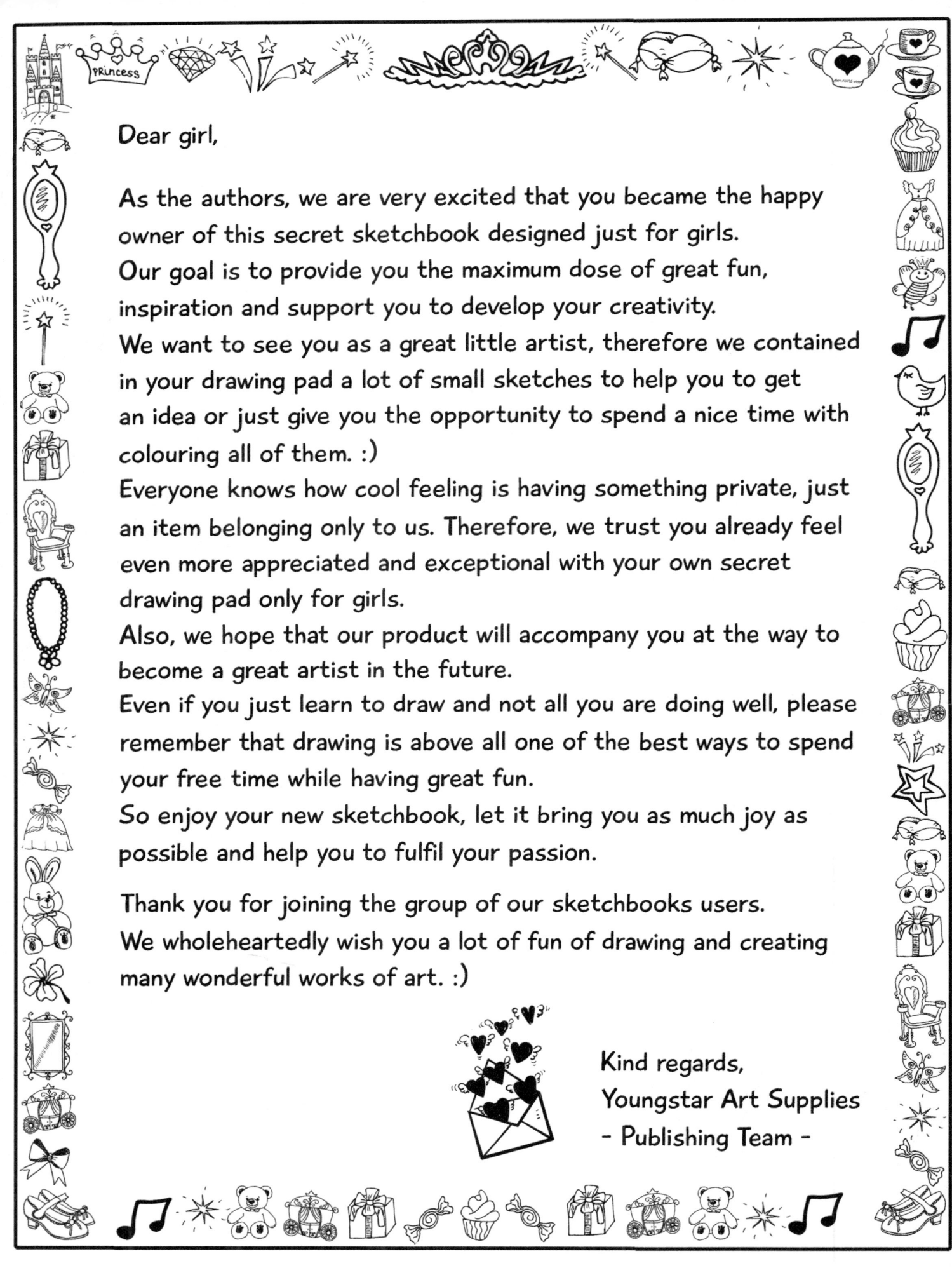

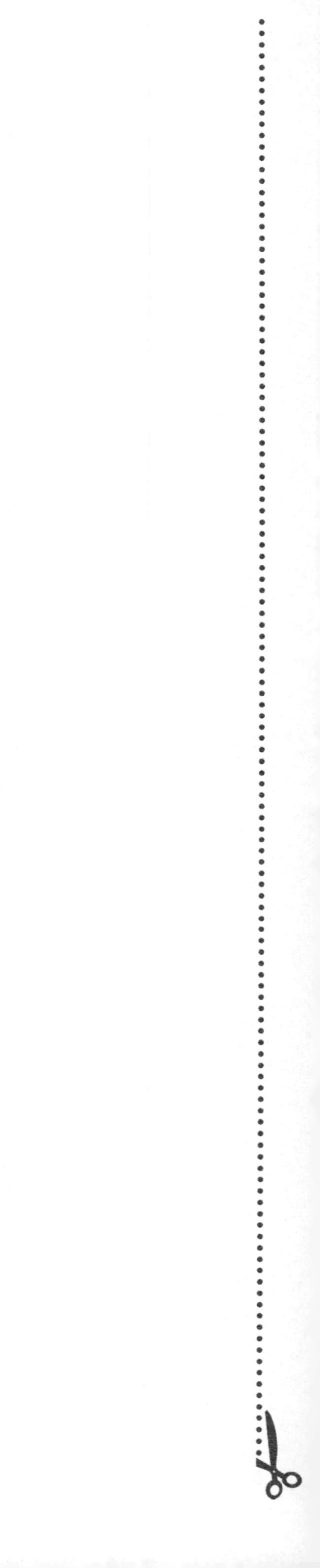

© Copyright by Youngstar Art Supplies. All rights reserved.

This publication is protected by copyright. No part of this book may be copied, reproduced or redistributed in any form without the express written consent and permission by the publisher.

Printed in Great Britain
by Amazon